EMMA LEARNS CREOLE

Action Words (Verbs)

BY NADINE COLLYMORE

Read

Cry

Sleep

Play

Sing

Talk

Eat

Run

Eat   Manje

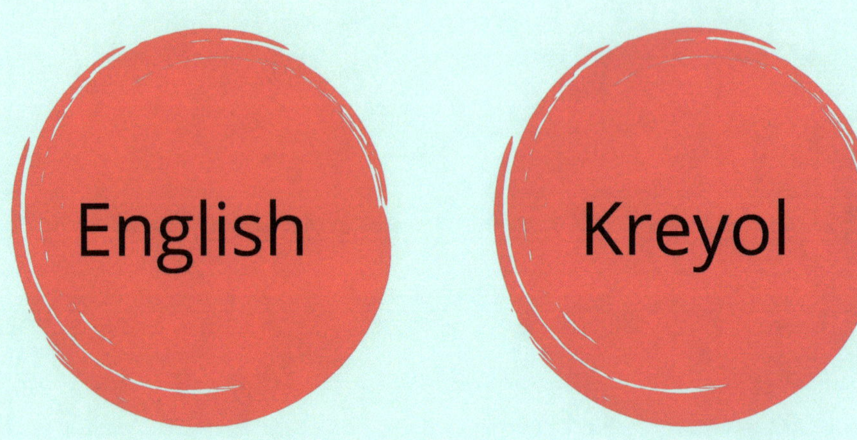

Run

Kouri

Dance   Danse

English

Kreyol

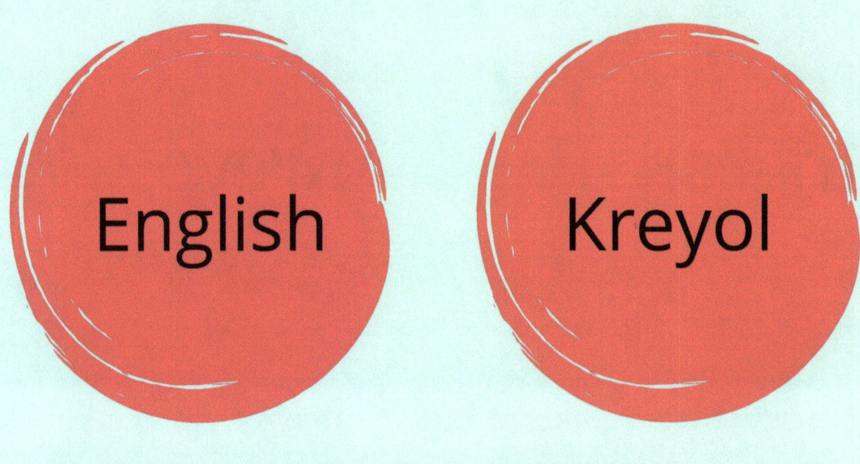

Sleep

Dòmi

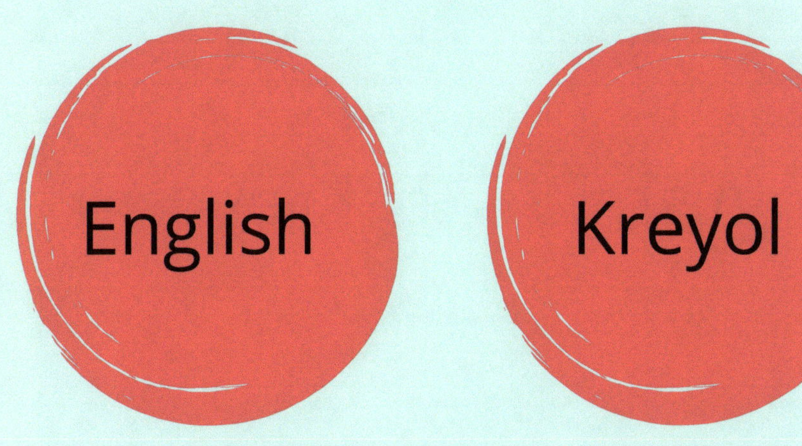

Climb Monte

Read

Ll

Play

Jwe

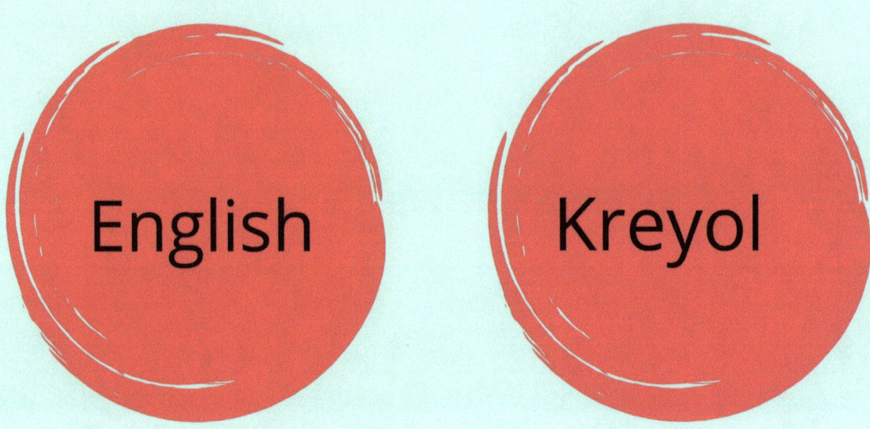

Laugh

Ri

Listen Koute

English | Kreyol

Walk | Mache

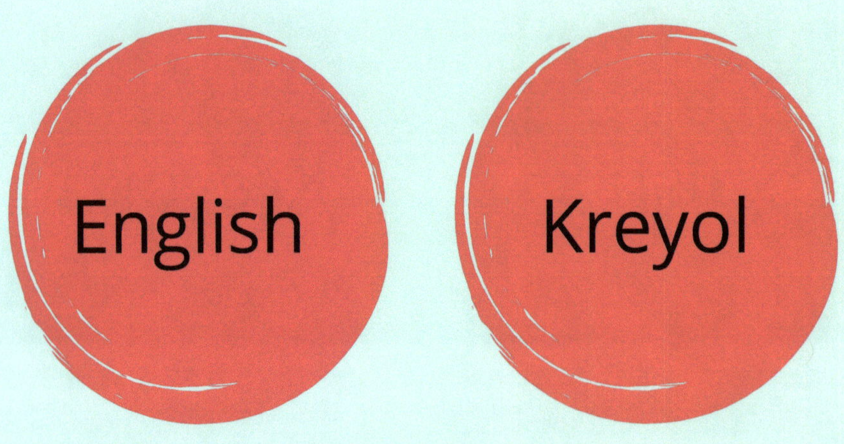

Speak   Pale

Cry

Kriye

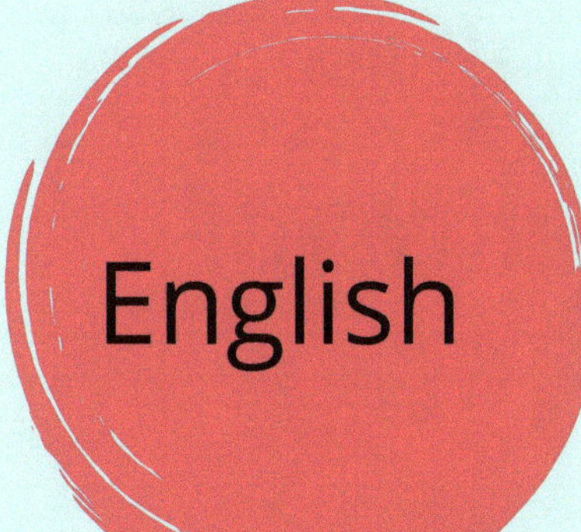

English	Kreyol
Jump	**Sote**

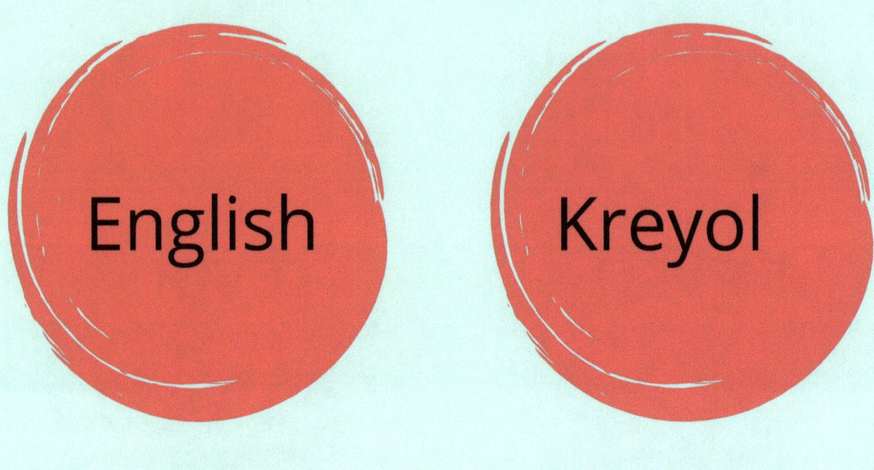

Fly   **Vole**

Drink   Bwè

Write

Ekri

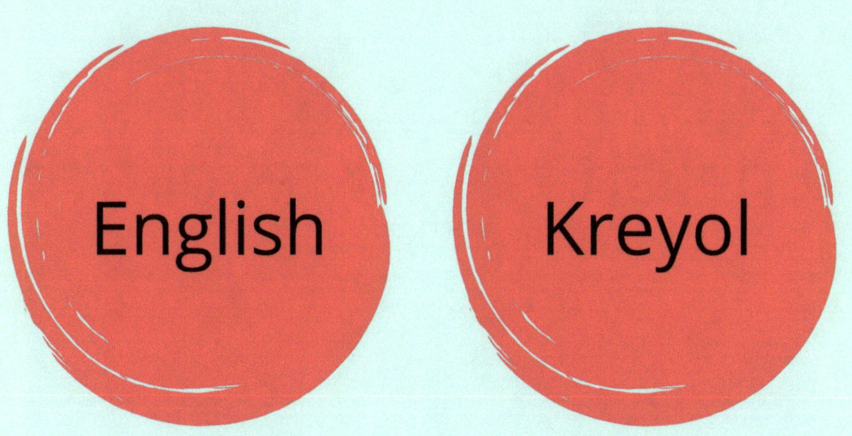

Sing Chante

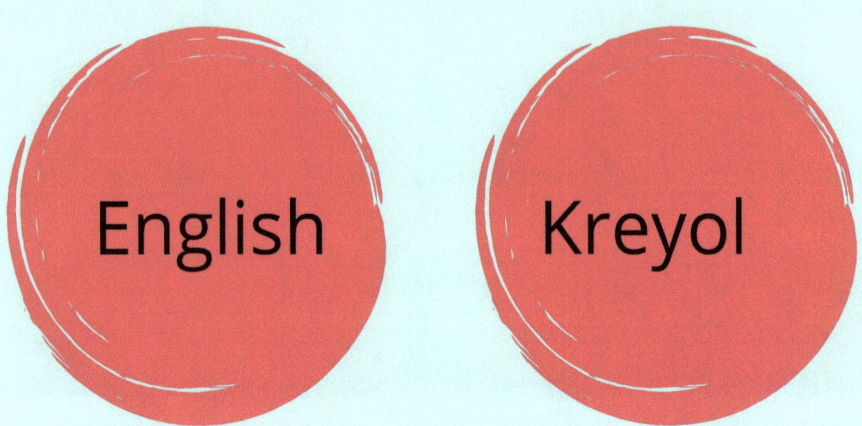

Shout   Rele

Paint Pentire

Study   Etidye

To my beautiful girls,
Nadia and Emma C.

This simple, fun book of verbs or words will teach you or your child a list of necessary verbs (words) typically used to complete a sentence in any Language. This picture book will help you develop your creole speaking skills by recognizing each word in both English and in Creole. It is perfectly illustrated to show the action of the words. Each picture tells you what the subject is doing in both languages.

It is a fun and easy way to learn a second language (creole)!